WISDOM

~~~

Wise Words to Live By

Compiled by
Lois J. Scott

Book Packager
Rev. Craig A. Narcisse

MCCLURE PUBLISHING, INC.
~~~

WISDOM

~~~

Wise Words to Live By

Compiled by
Lois J. Scott

Book Packager
Rev. Craig A. Narcisse
~~~

*THIS BOOK IS DEDICATED
TO EDNA BASS NARCISSE
WHOSE MEMORY WE
SHARE AND LOVE!*

*MAY THESE WISE WORDS
OF WISDOM INSPIRE YOU
TO GROW IN LOVE, PEACE,
HOPE, TRUTH, AND FAITH.*

FOREWORD

This book features a selection of clever words of wisdom, compiled by Lois J. Scott of Chicago, Illinois. Becoming an avid reader while reading books such as the Bible and many other books and magazines, contributed to her discernment of spiritual and wise sayings that she shares here with you.

Ms. Scott, a retired Chicago Public School teacher, has been a member of St. Thomas Episcopal Church for over thirty years. Read and indulge yourself in some of the wisdom she has absorbed.

She finally agreed to allow me to produce and publish this book that she dedicated to my mother, Edna, who was one of her best friends. I trust that these proverbial words of wisdom will inspire you to grow in love, peace, hope, truth, and faith.

Enjoy!

Reverend Craig A. Narcisse

= = = =

WISDOM
Wise Words to Live By

**As humans we are
never sinless, but as
Christians we
will sin less.**

~ ~ ~ ~

**The world is in this
wilderness because it
needs some learning,
training, and testing
time to grow.**

~ ~ ~ ~

**When you take your life
into your own hands,
you take God's hands
out of your life.**

~ ~ ~ ~

We must keep our motives to do good pleasing to God. He knows all our intentions and why.

~ ~ ~ ~

Excuses, excuses! The result of sin is to find someone else to blame.

~ ~ ~ ~

Listen to and study the Bible daily to get rid of attitudes and behaviors that keep us in conflict and disputes.

~ ~ ~ ~

Wishing and hoping accomplishes nothing if there is no action.

~ ~ ~ ~

"Self-righteous Christians" are victims of religion without a true relationship with God.

~ ~ ~ ~

Don't worry about tomorrow because tomorrow will worry about itself.

~ ~ ~ ~

Accusations must be supported by evidence before taking any disciplining action.

~ ~ ~ ~

Satan's demons will always have influence

in your life, but your
faith should never let
them possess your life.

~ ~ ~ ~

It is by prayer we ask
and receive answers,
but it is by being
thankful that God hears
and blesses us.

~ ~ ~ ~

Turn your worry list into
your prayer list. Don't
worry about anything
but pray
about everything!

~ ~ ~ ~

Always let love be
motivated by a pure

heart, a clear
conscience and
sincere faith.

~ ~ ~ ~

We have a choice:
either we live our lives
for what people think of
us or for what God
thinks of us.

~ ~ ~ ~

The one who loves you
completely is the one
who loves you
unconditionally.

~ ~ ~ ~

Change how you feel by
changing what you
are thinking.

~ ~ ~ ~

Good works don't save
a Christian, but shows a
Christian is saved!

~ ~ ~ ~

It is not always what we
are eating, but what is
eating us that we need
to deal with.

~ ~ ~ ~

True Christians don't
care about how much
you have, but how
much you care.

~ ~ ~ ~

Kind words turn away
wrath. Unkind words
stir up anger.

~ ~ ~ ~

**Don't set your
expectations of others
too high and you
won't ever get
too disappointed.**

~ ~ ~ ~

**Don't let anybody's
critical or angry
remarks rob you of your
good nature.**

~ ~ ~ ~

**You can't choose all the
circumstances that
come into your life, but
you can choose how to
respond to them.**

~ ~ ~ ~

It is easier to stay out of
trouble, than to get
out of trouble.

~ ~ ~ ~

The world can create
trouble in peace, but
God can create
peace in trouble.

~ ~ ~ ~

Courage is not the
absence of fear but
causes one to
triumph over it.

~ ~ ~ ~

Thank God, even
in adversity.

~ ~ ~ ~

**Praise God, He can give
you wisdom and power.
Wisdom to know what
to do and the power
to do it.**

~ ~ ~ ~

**A pessimist sees the
difficulty in every
opportunity. An
optimist sees the
opportunity in
every difficulty.**

~ ~ ~ ~

**To make sound
decisions, base them
on the best information
you get from all sides.**

The fool has it all wrong but is convinced he is right.

~ ~ ~ ~

Never interpret the Bible from your experiences, but interpret your experiences from the Bible.

~ ~ ~ ~

About the Bible: whatever is concealed in the Old Testament is revealed in the New Testament.

~ ~ ~ ~

Every time we get our feelings hurt and take

vengeful offense, we
play right into the
devil's hands.

~ ~ ~ ~

Worry is like a rocking
chair, it gives you
something to do but
accomplishes nothing.

~ ~ ~ ~

Sin will keep you from
the Bible, but the Bible
will keep you from sin.

~ ~ ~ ~

The great tragedy in life
is not death, but life
without purpose.

~ ~ ~ ~

The incorruptible seed is God's word.

~ ~ ~ ~

Don't tell God how big your problem is. Tell your problem how big your God is.

~ ~ ~ ~

We are not seeking the right thing when we seek the created thing first, rather seek the Creator first.

~ ~ ~ ~

Fear has a dead end. Faith has a future.

~ ~ ~ ~

Courage isn't having the strength to go on, but courage is going on even when you don't have the strength.

~ ~ ~ ~

The world can create trouble in peace. God can create peace in trouble.

~ ~ ~ ~

May the Lord continue to protect and guide us as a nation and shelter us under the shadow of His wings.

~ ~ ~ ~

The FOOL:

- ➢ Argues with the wise and listens to fools.
- ➢ Looks at what is foolish and sees it as wise.
- ➢ Has it all wrong but is sure he is right.
- ➢ Thinks he is slick when everyone else knows he is a fool.

~ ~ ~ ~

Our worst day with God is better than our best day without Him!

~ ~ ~ ~

Don't worry, the only
thing it changes is your
blood pressure.

~ ~ ~ ~

He who truly-believes,
obeys. He who obeys,
truly-believes.

~ ~ ~ ~

Don't worry about
anything but pray
about everything.

~ ~ ~ ~

If you search for good
you will find good.
If you search for evil,
evil will find you.

~ ~ ~ ~

**Pride leads to disgrace,
but with humility
comes wisdom.**

~ ~ ~ ~

**We are not saved by
good works, but for
good works.**

~ ~ ~ ~

**The Lord hates people
with twisted hearts,
but delights in those
who have integrity.**

~ ~ ~ ~

**With love in our hearts
let us approach God
with humility, others
with compassion, and
ourselves with respect
and integrity.**

~ ~ ~ ~

**Don't set your
expectations of others
too high
and you won't ever
become too
disappointed.**

~ ~ ~ ~

**True Christians don't
care about how much
you have, they care
about how much
you care.**

~ ~ ~ ~

**Hypocrites teach the
word of Christ but
disobey it themselves.**

~ ~ ~ ~

Sometimes God lets old
experiences come to an
end so that we may
begin new ones.

~ ~ ~ ~

The Holy Spirit enables
us to do the right
things, in the right way,
with the right motives.

~ ~ ~ ~

The one who loves you
completely is the
one who loves you
unconditionally.

~ ~ ~ ~

It is by prayer we ask
and receive answers;

**it is by being thankful,
God hears and
blesses us.**

~ ~ ~ ~

**We can't always choose
what happens to us,
but we can choose
how to respond.**

~ ~ ~ ~

**Sometimes when God
says no it is because He
has to bypass our plans
to get to His purpose.**

~ ~ ~ ~

**A lot of what happens
to us is not as
important as the
meaning we assign to it.**

~ ~ ~ ~

Witnessing is sharing our knowledge of the Bible with others, then leaving the results to God.

~ ~ ~ ~

Don't complain about the "thorns" of the roses, but see the "beauty" of the roses, despite their thorns.

~ ~ ~ ~

People may not always do what you want them to, but be thankful for the things they do anyway.

~ ~ ~ ~

Remember to judge the good as well as the bad when evaluating criticism.

~ ~ ~ ~

Represent yourself to others as you would to God.

~ ~ ~ ~

There is nothing like the beauty of a truthful and loving heart.

~ ~ ~ ~

God has not given us the spirit of fear, but the power of love and a sound mind.

~ ~ ~ ~

Don't worry about anything, but pray about everything with thanksgiving.

~ ~ ~ ~

Sometimes in judgment, even when we believe we are right, remember we can be wrong.

~ ~ ~ ~

Prayer lets us speak to God. Meditation lets God speak to us.

~ ~ ~ ~

Don't just talk about God, but walk in His ways.

~ ~ ~ ~

We must not love just in
words, but in actions
and truth.

~ ~ ~ ~

The beauty of creation
reflects the beauty of
our Creator.

~ ~ ~ ~

If we don't live for the
compliments of people,
we won't pay any
attention to their
negative criticism.

~ ~ ~ ~

Faith is the bridge
between the physical
and spiritual world.

~ ~ ~ ~

**If we daily feed our
spirit with God's word,
we will starve the sinful
nature of the flesh.**

~ ~ ~ ~

**Every moment we draw
a breath is a gift from
God – be thankful!**

~ ~ ~ ~

**Do everything for the
glory of God.**

~ ~ ~ ~

**The strength of the
church is the Christian.
The strength of the
Christian is the church.**

~ ~ ~ ~

To find God, we must be willing to seek Him.

~ ~ ~ ~

We can't do much about the faces we were born with, but we can do something about the person we are growing into.

~ ~ ~ ~

We measure time with clocks and calendars, but we remember time with our events in life.

~ ~ ~ ~

Be quicker to console and to encourage – and slower to judge.

~ ~ ~ ~

**Give God first place in
your life and
use time in a way that
pleases Him.**

~ ~ ~ ~

**The key to a happy life
and successful living is
right thinking, followed
by right action.**

~ ~ ~ ~

**We who are strong and
mature in God's word,
have won our battle
with Satan.**

~ ~ ~ ~

**Not every decision
involves a problem,**

but every problem involves a decision.

~ ~ ~ ~

Kind words turn away wrath. Unkind words stir up anger.

~ ~ ~ ~

Grace is not sweet until sin is bitter.

~ ~ ~ ~

We have a choice: either we live our lives for what people think of us or live for what God thinks of us.

~ ~ ~ ~

Never interpret the Bible from our

experiences but interpret our experiences from the Bible.

~ ~ ~ ~

Satan's demons will always have influence in your life, but your faith should never let them possess your life.

~ ~ ~ ~

If you don't love God and yourself, you can't love others – you can't give away what you don't have.

~ ~ ~ ~

Do we act the way we
are treated or are we
treated the way we act?

~ ~ ~ ~

Instead of looking
around and
complaining about what
we think, we need to
look around and thank
God for what we have.

~ ~ ~ ~

When the hand of God
comes off, the enemy
has free range.

~ ~ ~ ~

Life is not where we
came from, but where
we are going.

~ ~ ~ ~

Holding on to anger is like drinking poison and expecting the other person to die.

~ ~ ~ ~

To make sound decisions, base them on the best information you can get from all sides.

~ ~ ~ ~

Negative thoughts keep us from God's best blessings.

~ ~ ~ ~

A true friend is someone who reaches

for your hand but
touches your heart.

~ ~ ~ ~

We can't accurately
judge others unless we
truly know the motive of
our heart.

~ ~ ~ ~

Guilt tells us we've
done something wrong.
Shame says we are
something wrong.

~ ~ ~ ~

Nobody is perfect, so
we must learn to
tolerate each other's
imperfections.

~ ~ ~ ~

God's wisdom is shown to be right by the lives who follow it.

~ ~ ~ ~

Don't waste your breath on fools for they despise the wisest advice.

~ ~ ~ ~

If the Truth turns you off, examine yourself.

~ ~ ~ ~

Let's make sure that our thoughts are resisting the devil and not assisting him.

~ ~ ~ ~

Prayer is not about bending God's will so your will can be done, it's about bending your will so that God's Will is done.

~ ~ ~ ~

Judge not so that you will not be judged.

~ ~ ~ ~

Sometimes what is said is not rightfully heard. Words can be misinterpreted and misunderstood, so question their meaning.

~ ~ ~ ~

Success is getting what you want.

Happiness is being satisfied with what you get.

~ ~ ~ ~

When we seek things, we may miss the kingdom, but seek the kingdom and things will come.

~ ~ ~ ~

Keep believing and growing in faith. God will keep us to a better way of life.

~ ~ ~ ~

Even a fool may be thought wise if he keeps his mouth shut.

~ ~ ~ ~

The devil's way will
curse you. God's way
will bless you.
You have a choice!

~ ~ ~ ~

We can't fool God, so
choose Him by your
words and deeds.

~ ~ ~ ~

Recognize wrong
thoughts immediately,
and replace them with
God's thoughts.

~ ~ ~ ~

Give all of yourself to
God and He will give all
of Himself to you.

~ ~ ~ ~

Learning to listen to the
Holy Spirit within us,
will ensure that we are
guided into the
right action.

~ ~ ~ ~

Our lives will not be
valued by what we take,
but by what we give.

~ ~ ~ ~

To help do the right
thing always seek the
Holy Spirit's enabling
power through prayer.

~ ~ ~ ~

The devil wants us to be
fault finding of others,
so that we don't have to

see or deal with our
own faults.

~ ~ ~ ~

If we keep our minds
from thinking evil, our
eyes from seeing evil,
our ears from hearing
evil, our tongue will
speak no evil.

~ ~ ~ ~

Give what you want to,
not what you have to.
Everyone loves a
cheerful giver.

~ ~ ~ ~

God searches us and
knows the motives of
our heart and thoughts.

~ ~ ~ ~

Don't beat around the
bush; say what you
mean and mean what
you say!

~ ~ ~ ~

It is considered evil to
do a good deed for the
wrong motive.

~ ~ ~ ~

Mature believers know
how to make the best of
a bad situation.
When life gives you a
lemon, make lemonade.

~ ~ ~ ~

We must trade in our
own self-righteousness

for the new
righteousness of Christ,
by faith.

~ ~ ~ ~

The love of God, the
grace of Jesus, and the
fellowship of the Holy
Spirit will strengthen us
as we obey His Word.

~ ~ ~ ~

Do nothing from selfish
ambition or conceit, but
in humility and
unselfishness
consider others.

~ ~ ~ ~

We must keep our
motives to do good,
pleasing to God.

**He knows all of our
intentions and why.**

~ ~ ~ ~

**Always expect the
unexpected and prepare
for those events.
Have a plan B!**

~ ~ ~ ~

**Immature Christians
dwell on the negative
things in life.
Mature Christians dwell
on the positive things.**

~ ~ ~ ~

**To get the real TRUTH,
let's question our
motives. Ask, what
would Jesus do or say?**

~ ~ ~ ~

As we immerse ourselves in God's Word, let us live our lives by being controlled by the power of the Holy Spirit that lives in us.

~ ~ ~ ~

Why do we seem to focus on the negative in people and things when there is so much good in them?

~ ~ ~ ~

Listen to and read the Bible daily to get rid of attitudes and behaviors that keep us in conflicts and disputes.

~ ~ ~ ~

Bad attitudes cause bad behavior.

~ ~ ~ ~

We should not let selfish motives, motivate our "so-called" good deeds.

~ ~ ~ ~

Living under grace is not the license to do what you want to, but the moral reason to do what you spiritually should.

~ ~ ~ ~

Put on the whole armor of God because the devil is still looking for

our weakness to sneak
in and devour us.

~ ~ ~ ~

Our word is our bond
only when we have a
track record of honesty
and integrity regarding
what we say and do.

~ ~ ~ ~

Remember, our
omniscient God knows
and sees all of our
thoughts and motives.

~ ~ ~ ~

Self-righteous
Christians are victims
of religion without a
true relationship with
God.

~ ~ ~ ~

An awareness of the debt of sin Christ paid for us, should motivate us to lavish him with extreme self-sacrificing love.

~ ~ ~ ~

We display the fruit of the Spirit of God when we are:

1. Constantly loving with difficult people,
2. Joyful in trying times,
3. Gentle instead of harsh and argumentative,
4. Thinking of the needs of others

instead of ourselves
when making
decisions, and
5. Peaceful regardless
of the circumstances.

~ ~ ~ ~

There is no truer friend
than a friend who
defends his friend from
idle gossip, heard or
said about him
or others.

~ ~ ~ ~

To be content and
satisfied with what you
have and do, practice
these things: love,
peace, kindness,
self-control, patience,
thankfulness, gratitude,

**forgiveness, and
faith in God.**

~ ~ ~ ~

**Accusations must be
supported by evidence
before taking
disciplinary action.**

~ ~ ~ ~

**Live and enjoy the life
you have now, until you
do what others have
done to enjoy the life
they have now.**

~ ~ ~ ~

**Be grateful,
THANK GOD!**

~ ~ ~ ~

You can't please all the
people all the time;
even if you can't please
most of the people most
of the time, strive to
please God all the time
– hoping this happens
most of the time.
~ ~ ~ ~

Do not worry about
tomorrow, for tomorrow
will worry about itself.
~ ~ ~ ~

We need to keep our
mind plugged into the
power of the
Holy Spirit – so that it
works in us, giving us
the desire and passion
always to please God.
~ ~ ~ ~

Whatever things are lovely, pleasant, kind, spiritual, peaceful, good, and nice, think on these things at all times.

~ ~ ~ ~

God wants us to use things and love people, not to love things and use people.

~ ~ ~ ~

Change how you feel by changing what you think.

~ ~ ~ ~

Expose yourself daily to positive things in life.

~ ~ ~ ~

**Master your emotions
by listening to and
reading the Word
of God.**

~ ~ ~ ~

**Give thanks for our
caregivers everywhere
for putting their lives on
the line for others
during times of need.**

~ ~ ~ ~

**The great tragedy in life
is not death, but life
without purpose.**

~ ~ ~ ~

**Good works don't save
a Christian, but shows a
Christian is saved.**

~ ~ ~ ~

You can't choose all the circumstances that come into your life, but you can choose whether they make you better or bitter.

~ ~ ~ ~

Don't let anybody's anger or critical remarks rob you of your sunny disposition or good nature.

~ ~ ~ ~

Fear has a dead end. Faith has a future.

~ ~ ~ ~

In order to succeed
in life:

1. Know who you are,
2. Take responsibility
   for your life,
3. Determine (choose)
   your priorities
   (values), and
4. Persevere with
   God's help even
   when things get
   difficult.

~ ~ ~ ~

God give us wisdom
and power: wisdom to
know what to do, and
the power to do it.

The world can create trouble in peace, but God can create peace in trouble.

~ ~ ~ ~

Always listen for God's Holy Spirit. His wisdom is working in, through, and for you. Yield to it and let it lead and guide you.

~ ~ ~ ~

A good sermon is like a mini skirt: short enough to be interesting and long enough to cover the essentials.

~ ~ ~ ~

**When I trust God to
meet my needs, I stop
worrying about things
and turning my care
to others.**

~ ~ ~ ~

**Don't put all your hope
in wealth but be rich in
good deeds.
You cannot serve God
and money too.**

~ ~ ~ ~

**As we carefully nourish
our flesh with food
daily, let us
also carefully nourish
our spirit with the Word
of God, daily!**

~ ~ ~ ~

Let the Lord:
- ➢ **Give you wisdom.**
- ➢ **Guide your walk.**
- ➢ **Guard your way.**

~ ~ ~ ~

When reading God's word, keep your mind alert and your heart receptive.

~ ~ ~ ~

Accept the things you can't change, change the things you can, and be wise enough to know the difference.

~ ~ ~ ~

We receive true joy when the Lord pours out His grace to us.

~ ~ ~ ~

The word of the Lord is
an incorruptible seed.
Sow it into your mind
and heart; it will
produce a
good harvest.

~ ~ ~ ~

Don't make a career out
of your problems.

~ ~ ~ ~

Our lives will be valued
not by what we take, but
what we give.

~ ~ ~ ~

Rejoice in the Lord, for
a merry heart does
good like medicine.

~ ~ ~ ~

The Lord is moved by your needs, but He responds to your faith.

~ ~ ~ ~

Trust Him: take your hands off the wheel and let God take you where you should go!

~ ~ ~ ~

It is okay to be concerned, but when you mix concern with anxiety you get, worry.

~ ~ ~ ~

True peace, comfort, and reassurance comes from the Holy Spirit

dwelling in and
guiding us.

~ ~ ~ ~

If all our thoughts are of
kindness and peace,
our hearts will speak
only of love and truth.

~ ~ ~ ~

At the end of our earthly
journey, may we
continue into our
eternal home.

~ ~ ~ ~

Life is full of ups and
downs, but reading
God's Word help us up
the downs.

~ ~ ~ ~

The truly educated
person never
stops learning.

~ ~ ~ ~

Every day is not a good
day, but if you look, you
can find something
good in the day.

~ ~ ~ ~

If we resent others
when they don't meet
our needs, it may be
because we are
insensitive to
their needs.

~ ~ ~ ~

Regrets are a waste of
time when there is so

much love, beauty, and humor in the world.

~ ~ ~ ~

Always be open-minded in your listening, speaking, and thinking.

~ ~ ~ ~

Don't let your service to the things of the church let you forget your service to the God of the church.

~ ~ ~ ~

Understanding the wisdom of the Bible results in good judgment.

~ ~ ~ ~

God's spirit helps us in our weakness. It convicts us and helps us see sin as it really is.

~ ~ ~ ~

Through the Holy Spirit we are influenced by God to overcome evil with good.

~ ~ ~ ~

The Lord listens to us when we pray and grants those things that help us to walk in His ways.

~ ~ ~ ~

Can't you just be happy for me?

~ ~ ~ ~

**A heart full of gratitude
causes a joyful attitude.**

~ ~ ~ ~

**A joyful attitude comes
from a heart full
of gratitude.**

~ ~ ~ ~

**Life is shorter than you
think, so learn to be
content in any situation.**

~ ~ ~ ~

**When we go to church,
we know the building,
but do we know
the Builder?**

~ ~ ~ ~

**Love yourself; you can't
give away what you
don't have.**

~ ~ ~ ~

**As food nourishes your
body, the Bible
nourishes your spirit.**
~ ~ ~ ~

**God has forgiven you
for your sins.
Have you
forgiven yourself?**
~ ~ ~ ~

**True love does not
seek its own!**
~ ~ ~ ~

**As much as it depends
on you, live in peace.**
~ ~ ~ ~

These words of
wisdom to live by
compiled by
Lois J. Scott
of Chicago, Illinois,
reminds us that it is
better to be wise
than foolish.

Ms. Scott is a
member of
Saint Thomas
Episcopal Church
and a retired
schoolteacher.